Egypt · Eritrea · Syria

RED EAGLES

THE STORY OF THE 4th INDIAN DIVISION

Tunisia · Italy · Greece

The Naval & Military Press Ltd

Published by

The Naval & Military Press Ltd
Unit 5 Riverside, Brambleside
Bellbrook Industrial Estate
Uckfield, East Sussex
TN22 1QQ England

Tel: +44 (0)1825 749494

www.naval-military-press.com

In reprinting in facsimile from the original, any imperfections are inevitably reproduced and the quality may fall short of modern type and cartographic standards.

4th INDIAN DIVISION PICTO

Bizerte
Tunis
Enfidaville
Sousse
M E D I T E R R A N E
Sfax
Gabes
Medenine
Zwara
Tripoli
Benghazi
Gulf of
Sidra
Sirte
TRIPOLITANIA

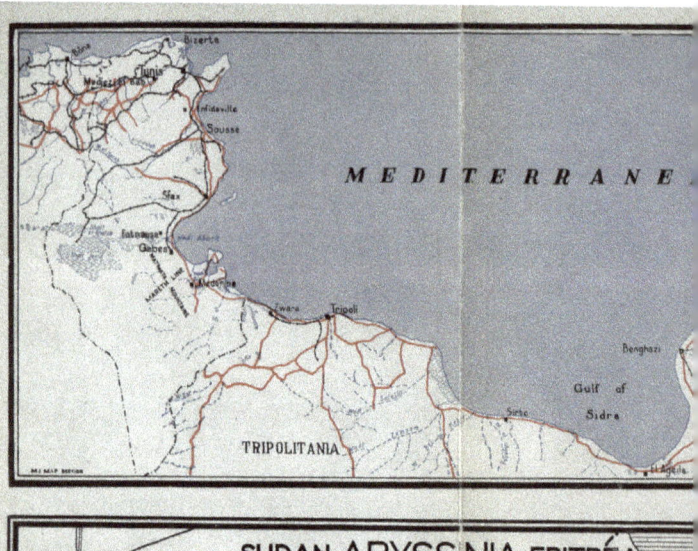

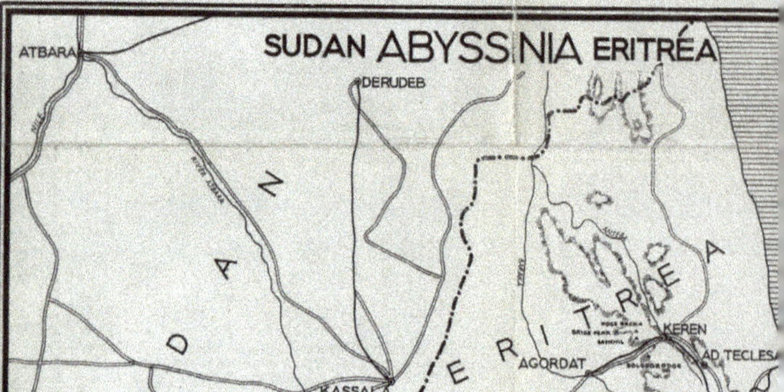
SUDAN ABYSSINIA ERITRÉA
ATBARA
DERUDEB
S U D A N
E R I T R E A
KEREN
AD TECLESA
AGORDAT
KASSALA
ACIOTA
BARENTU
ASMARA
KHASHM
EL GIRBA
GEDAREF
GALLABAT
GONDAR
A B Y S S I
LEGEND
RAILWAY
ROADS
RIVERS
DIVISIONAL ROUTE
BATTLE

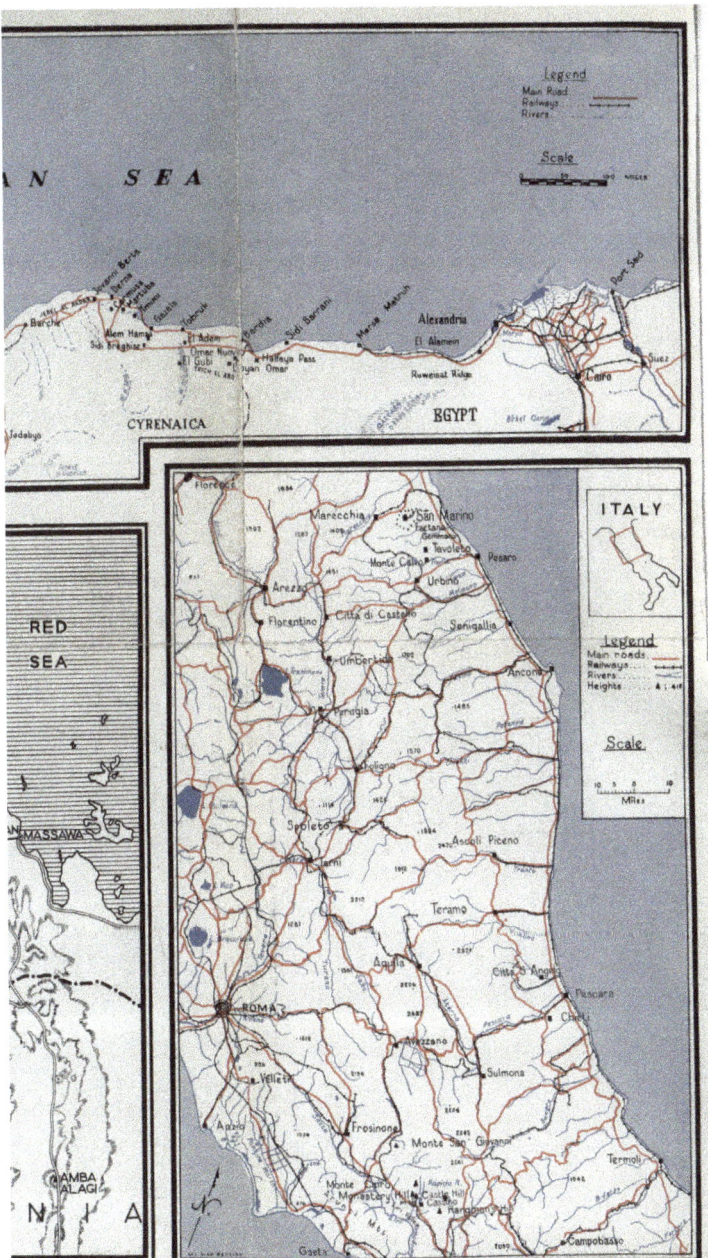

To

7th BRITISH ARMOURED DIVISION

and

2nd NEW ZEALAND DIVISION

... Our Oldest Comrades

LEFT :
Maj. Gen. (now Lt. Gen. Sir) F. I. S. TUKER, K.C.I.E., C.B., C.B.E., D.S.O., Commanded Feb. 1942 until March 1944.

OTHER COMMANDERS

Maj. Gen. (now Lt. Gen. Sir) N. M. de la P. BERESFORD PIERSE, K.B.E., C.B., D.S.O., commanded May 1940 until April 1941.

Maj. Gen. (now Lt. Gen. Sir) F. W. MESSERVY, K.B.E., C.B., D.S.O., commanded April 1941 until Feb 1942.

Maj. Gen. A. W. W. HOLWORTHY, D.S.O., M.C., commanded March until Dec. 1944.

Maj. Gen. C. H. BOUCHER C.B C.B.E., D.S.O., commanded Jan until Dec. 1945.

BRIGADE COMMANDERS

RIGHT. Brig. J. C. SAUNDERS JACOBS, C.B.E., D.S.O., commanded the 5th Infantry Brigade.

ABOVE Brig. (now Maj. Gen.) O. de T. LOVETT, C.B.E., D.S.O., commanded the 7th Infantry Brigade.

RIGHT Brig. H. C. J. HUNT, C.B.E., D.S.O., commanded the 11th Infantry Brigade.

THE VICTORIA CROSS

Subedar RICHPAL RAM, 4/6th Rajputana Rifles, won his V.C. during an attack on Keren. Posthumous.

Subedar (now Sub-Maj.) LALBAHADUR THAPA, 1/2nd Gurkha Rifles, awarded the V.C. for gallantry in Tunisia.

Coy. Hav. Maj. CHHELU RAM, 4/6th Rajputana Rifles, won the V.C. for gallantry in Tunisia. Posthumous.

Rifleman SHER BAHADUR THAPA, 1/9th Gurkha Rifles, at Faetano in Italy, charged an enemy position under persistent small arms fire, killing a machine gunner and putting the remainder to flight. Later, he silenced several more machine gun posts, and was killed rescuing two wounded men. He was posthumously awarded the V.C.

THE GEORGE CROSS

RIGHT:
Lieut. St. J. G. YOUNG, Central India Horse, was in command of a patrol in Italy, which encountered a minefield; a number of men were wounded. Later, with one leg blown off and another shattered, whilst crawling to the assistance of a wounded sowar to apply a field dressing, he showed his patrol how to extricate themselves. He was posthumously awarded the George Cross.

Sowar DITTO RAM, Central India Horse, was a member of the patrol commanded by Lt. Young. On the explosion of a Schu mine he was among 5 men wounded.
Despite this, he crawled through the minefield to assist another injured man, fully aware of the danger. He died a few minutes after having bandaged his comrade's wounds. This young soldier was posthumously awarded the George Cross.

Subedar SUBRAMANYAN, I.D.S.M., Q.V.O., Madras Sappers and Miners. For flinging himself on top of a mine which was about to explode during the battle for Monastery Hill, and thereby saving the lives of several of his comrades for the sacrifice of his own, this soldier was posthumously awarded the George Cross, the first in the Division.

The 4th Indian Division in Italy

5th INDIAN INFANTRY BRIGADE

1/4th Bn. Essex Regiment. 1/6th Rajputana Rifles. 1/9th Gurkha Rifles. 3/10th Baluch Regiment.

7th INDIAN INFANTRY BRIGADE

1st Bn. Royal Sussex Regiment. 4/16th Punjab Regiment. 1/2nd Gurkha Rifles. 2/11th Sikh Regiment.

11th INDIAN INFANTRY BRIGADE

2nd Bn. Cameron Highlanders. 4/6th Rajputana Rifles. 2/7th Gurkha Rifles. 3/12th Frontier Force Regiment.

DIVISIONAL CAVALRY

Central India Horse.

MACHINE GUN BATTALION

Machine Gun Battalion Rajputana Rifles.

ARTILLERY

1st Field Regiment, R.A. 11th Field Regiment R.A. 31st Field Regiment R.A. 149th Anti-Tank Regiment R.A. 57th Light A.A. Regiment, R.A.

ENGINEERS

4th Field Company, Sappers and Miners. 12th Field Company, Sappers and Miners. 21st Field Company, Sappers and Miners. 11th Field Park Company, Sappers and Miners. 5th Bridging Platoon, Sappers and Miners.

MEDICAL SERVICES

17th Field Ambulance. 26th Field Ambulance. 32nd Field Ambulance. 15th Indian Field Hygiene Section.

MISCELLANEOUS

Divisional and Brigade Supply and Transport Companies, Divisional and Brigade Group Companies and Ordnance Field Parks, Divisional Signals, Postal Services, Provost Units, Security Sections.

 # RED EAGLES

"IT WAS PROPER that we should have worn eagles upon our shoulders, for only birds could have visited so many lands, or could have soared to some of the places where we fought. We went first, and armies sprang up behind us. The tally of those whom we slew was likewise that of an army. We captured many lakhs of prisoners, and as they marched away, their columns stretched over the horizon. Of our men, we left the strength of two divisions upon our battlefields. Jo Hukam."

So will run the tale in a hundred villages, to the circles of elders and to wide-eyed children in the shade. Nor like many veterans' tales, will it have grown unreasonably in stature. It is a matter of record that at one time 4 Ind. Div. was the only Allied Infantry formation in the Mediterranean theatre. The "Game Book" of the Division, which kept the score of men, tanks, guns and aircraft, shows what a multiple toll it took; yet this one Division suffered over 25,000 casualties. It captured more than 100,000 prisoners, and in nine campaigns travelled more than 15,000 miles. Nevertheless, such figures reveal less of the achievement of 4 Ind. Div. than their proud phrase, "Jo Hukam." Whatever was ordered, that thing we did."

There was still peace, but the shadow of war hung over the world, when the first units of 4 Ind. Div. arrived in Middle East. They came as part of a tiny force to garrison an Imperial cross-road. They were under French Supreme Command, for they were but a handful compared with the

French armies which confronted a quarter million Italians in East Africa, three hundred thousand Italians in Libya. Then broke that terrible day in June, 1940, when France fell with the Italian knife in her back. 4 Ind. Div. and Seventh Armoured Division held Egypt, but encircled by a half million enemies.

At that time, "Jo Hukam" might have seemed a silly boast, yet its phrase had already kindled a great resolve in the minds of soldiers. When Graziani was slow in invading Egypt, the garrison moved towards him. By September 1940, the Italians had only advanced forty miles from their frontier, whereas British and Indian troops had traversed two hundred and fifty miles of desert to meet them. The enemy was concentrated in a cluster of encampments to the south of Sidi Barrani. Three Italians faced one British or Indian soldier. Yet the invaders were already beleaguered in their perimeters, and General Wavell was intent on their destruction.

The battle of Sidi Barrani, between December 6th and December 10th, was one of the most complete victories of all time. To the freedom-loving nations of the world it came as a tonic and an inspiration to discover that Great Britain, standing alone save for her Commonwealth and Empire, and with British cities under fire, could yet strike such a deadly blow. It was the 4 Ind. Div's. battle for their comrades of

THE BUFFS (Royal East Kent Regt)

the Seventh Armoured Division, in their own words, were mostly occupied in "keeping the ring". First the Nibeiwa, then the Tummar, and finally the Sidi Barrani groups of camps were stormed in audacious but well-calculated assaults. In four days four enemy divisions were destroyed, and over 20,000 prisoners taken, for the loss of 700 men.

While the battle was in progress, news arrived that the Italians had invaded the Sudan. General Wavell was compelled to divide his sparse forces and to despatch 4 Ind. Div. in all haste to East Africa. On January 19th, the first Indian units arrived at Kassala, 250 miles east of Khartoum. Without waiting for comrades, 2nd Camerons, 4/11th Sikhs and 4/6th Rajputana Rifles hurried off to clear the upper of two roads leading into Eritrea. At Keru the Sikhs climbed the mountain and forced a stubbornly held position. Further to the east the road junction of Agordat was covered by a crescent of hills and ridges. The remainder of 4 Ind. Div. had now arrived and when the attack went in on January 28th, 3/14th Punjabs seized Mount Cochen, the dominating peak. Stiff fighting followed, involving 1/6th Rajputana Rifles and Bengal Sappers and Miners, who fought as infantry. When the high ground had been secured, the Camerons, 1st Royal Fusiliers and 1/2nd Punjabs exploited the gains. By January 31st the enemy was in full retreat

THE ROYAL FUSILIERS

to Keren, the gateway to Eritrea.

In the months that followed, Keren, like Sidi Barrani, became a name known around the world. It described a mountain range crowned by many sheer pinnacles, which stood sentinel before the Eritrean uplands. Only a narrow gorge afforded passage through this formidable barrier. 4 and 5 Ind. Divs. laboriously seized the lower spurs as a start line for assault on the high peaks, with the object of working along the summits until they could dominate Keren Gorge.

The Italians never fought better than in their defence of this massive position, which they believed to be impregnable. More than once gallant and desperate assaults won to the key heights, only to leave their dead there when fierce counter-attacks hurled the assailants back down the slopes. On Brigs Peak a company of Royal Fusiliers was reduced to eight men. On Mount Sammana the Camerons had only thirty men left. On Hogs Back 1/6th Rajputana Rifles lost 50% of their effectives. In an attack on Acqua Col, on the extreme right of the position, 4/6th Rajputana Rifles, which was destined to earn a mighty name, won its first Victoria Cross when Subedar Richpal Ram, with only a handful of his company remaining, battled to the death to hold the crests so hardly won.

THE ROYAL SUSSEX REGT.

Day and night the grim struggle continued. Finally 5 Ind. Div. was able to seize Dologorodoc, a feature half way up the main range, which commanded the entrance to Keren Gorge. On the night of March 26th, in a great attack, five battalions of this fine division burst through along slopes of the ravine and captured high ground at its far end. Next morning Keren surrendered. Except for some mopping up along the Red Sea littoral in which 7th Brigade participated, with 4/16th Punjabs breaking the resistance outside Massawa and being among the first unit to enter the Eritrean capital, the East African campaign had ended for 4 Ind. Div.

ERITREA

MULE TRANSPORT.
Nearly all vital supplies had to be provided by this method.

KEREN FROM HAPPY VALLEY — BRIG'S PEAK, SANCHIL, DOLOGORODOC, CAMERON RIDGE

AGORDAT. Abandoned by the enemy after the seizure of the Cochen area. Huge quantities of war material were captured here.

"HELL FIRE" CORNER

KEREN country. A glimpse of the mountainous terrain.

MASSAWA. 4/16th Punjabs were among the first troops to enter.

There was no rest, for now threats loomed in Middle East. Rommel's Afrika Korps was arriving in the Western Desert to stiffen the shaken Italians; in Syria, Vichy officials connived at German infiltration. In mid-June a force of 5th Brigade, Australians and Fighting French pushed up from the Sea of Tiberias towards Damascus. The Vichy French fought bitterly. At Kissoue 3/1st Punjabs and 4/6th Rajputanas stormed a position of such strength that a captured officer said, "That what you have done, it is unbelievable." On the evening of June 19th, elements of the same two battalions set out on a hazardous enterprise. They passed through the enemy lines in the dark, and seized the village of Mezze, where the road to the sea coast enters the Lebanon. Intense and deadly street fighting followed. The greatly outnumbered Rajputanas made a last stand in the village chateau. Although a relief column thrust up next afternoon, led by British gunners with their muzzles down, shooting their way through, it arrived too late to save the remnants, who had been overwhelmed by tanks and field guns firing at fifty yards range. The sacrifice, however, had not been in vain. Next day Damascus fell and for 5th Indian Brigade the Syrian campaign was over.

On almost the same date 11th Brigade was committed to no less critical an encounter on the Halfaya escarpment which marks the boundary between Egypt and Libya. An ambitious plan called for the capture of this strong position by twin attacks from the south and east. "Escarpment Force", consisting of a Royal Tank Regiment and a Guards Brigade, was briefed for this operation. At the outset the attack of

"Escarpment Force" was successful, but before the Halfaya garrisons could be destroyed, German panzers came rushing up and mauled the lighter British tanks. This action left the defenders free to deal with the frontal attack of "Coast Force". For thirty-six hours Camerons, 2/5th Mahrattas and 4/6th Rajputanas suffered heavily as they battled up and along the steep, wadi-ribbed wall of the escarpment. By the end of the second day the battered battalions were within five hundred yards of Halfaya Pass. As they drew together for a last surge, word came that only a narrow corridor remained through which "Escarpment Force" might withdraw, and that the operation was to be abandoned as a gallant but costly failure.

During the summer of 1941, 5th and 7th Brigades returned to the Western Desert to complete 4 Ind. Div. On the morning of November 18th, when the invasion of Libya was launched, the Indians and the New Zealanders led the van of the great fleets of vehicles which cruised across the frontier, seeking the enemy. At the Omars, two mere humps in the plain 22 miles south of Halfaya, 7th Brigade encountered well-sited and strongly held defences. The Royal Sussex with a superb rush accounted for Omar Nuovo, but in a similar attack on Libyan Omar 4/16th Punjabs lost most of their tanks and failed to win home. Rommel's armour raided into the east, temporarily disorganizing the advance. Near the Omars, 1st Field Regiment of 4 Ind. Div. was charged by twenty-five panzers. Although the guns were in the open, they more than held their own in a slogging match which cost the enemy eight tanks. That evening, with the garrison of Omar Nuovo standing on their vehicles like spectators at a race meeting, the German armour again tried to overrun the guns, an attempt which left eleven flaming derelicts on the plain.

5th and 11th Brigades had now come up, and 3/1st Punjabs joined with the 4/16th Punjabs in putting an end to Libyan Omar. At the cost of 336 casualties these Punjabi battalions destroyed a garrison of 3,000 men. Cunning co-operation between Central India Horse and New Zealand artillery won a succession of small fights further north and the enemy retired into his boltholes of Halfaya and Bardia. 11th Brigade now moved westwards into the desert along the dust-filled ruts of the ancient Road of Slaves and encounterred strong enemy forces near El Gubi, thirty-five miles south of Tobruk. Confused fighting ensued in which the adversaries were inextricably intermingled, and equally blinded by incessant dust storms. Fleets of vehicles blundered into deadly clashes or missed each other by yards in the murk. After two days, the enemy cried quits, and made off to the north-west. Tobruk was relieved and 4 Ind. Div. was entrusted with the pursuit through the Jebel Achdar, that fertile boss of high ground which fronts the Mediterranean for one hundred and forty miles between Tmemi and Benghazi. Pressing forward in desert columns the enemy

THE WELCH REGIMENT

was found in strength on a crescent line covering the entrance to the bottleneck through which he must retreat. He turned and lashed viciously at his pursuers. On December 14th, thirty-nine panzers tried to overrun 7th Brigade at Sidi Breghise but were beaten off by the gallantry of 25th Field Regiment. Next day, at Alem Hamza, came disaster. Fight to the last, 31st Field Regiment and 1st Buffs, which had replaced Royal Fusiliers in 5th Brigade, were overrun and destroyed by a "bull's rush" of self-propelled guns and panzers.

South African, New Zealand, British and Polish divisions were closing up, and the enemy dropped back through the Jebel closely pursued by two Indian brigades. On December 18th, by taking a short cut across country, 4/11th Sikhs emerged from road-side undergrowth to sweep in on Derna airfield, Wild West fashion, shooting up the aircraft, including twelve Junkers troop carriers which settled down during the battle. 183 aircraft were captured or destroyed. 5th Brigade essayed even more difficult cross-country navigation, and cut the main line of the retreat securing 650 prisoners at the cost of one killed and five wounded. Thereafter the enemy stood briefly at Giovanni Berta, but with Central India Horse harassing well ahead, the pursuit maintained its momentum. Benghazi was reached on Christmas Eve. Rommel had withdrawn to his old stronghold in the marshes

at the bottom of the Gulf of Sirte, and Libya was cleansed of the enemy.

A substantial victory had been won with sparse forces. This thinness on the ground presented Major-General F.I.S. Tuker, who took command from Major-General F. W. Messervy on New Year's Day, with a division strung out over 125 miles of broken country and dependent upon two rain-sodden desert tracks for communications. Moreover, it was evident that although the Germans had been roughly handled, they were still full of fight, and their armour in particular was battleworthy. Trouble was near at hand, for on January 21st a fleet of 3,000 vehicles sallied out of Agheila, and headed swiftly into the north-west, across the chord of the Jebel.

It was obvious that unless the desert to the south was under control, the Jebel was indefensible. Some indecision prevailed. On January 28th, as twilight fell, German tanks lurched out of the undergrowth and lumbered down towards the roads leading eastwards from Benghazi. 57th L.A.A. Regiment, the toast of the Division because of its skill in picking Stukas out of the skies, blasted the leading panzers to scrap metal, but others swept on and established road blocks. A gallant attempt to break through failed and 7th Indian Brigade, with Central India Horse and detachments of

THE CAMERON HIGHLANDERS

gunners, was sealed up in the seaport. Fortunately Brigadier Briggs was a cool and canny fighter. His forces were already organized in desert columns, and with the advantage of a stormy night three groups—Gold Group, Silver Group and Headquarters Group—slipped through the enemy cordon to the south of Benghazi and swung eastwards in a long detour through the depths of the desert. Experience and foresight countered every hazard and after some exciting passages, 4,100 men came to safety, with less than 100 lost.

5th Brigade meanwhile dropped back along the Jebel roads, fighting skilful rearguard actions and avoiding encirclement by well-timed withdrawals. As it neared safety the enemy managed to outpace the retirement and at Carmusa closed from three sides on 11th Brigade columns, which were covering the vital Martuba road junction through which 5th Brigade must withdraw. By dour and skilful fighting, in perhaps the most brilliant defensive engagement in Divisional history, the Camerons, the Mahrattas and 144th Field Regiment held back the enemy until 5th Brigade was safe.

On February 4th, 4 Ind. Div. came into the new British lines at Gazala. It was relieved and promptly disintegrated. 7th Brigade went to Cyprus, 5th Brigade to Palestine, and 11th Brigade to Egypt.

There they lay in the latter half of May, when it became

evident that Rommel had won the race in Libya, and would be first to attack. 11th Brigade, which had been training for an amphibious operation on the Tripolitanian Coast, hurried to the Western Desert early in June, when the battle turned against the Eighth Army. With the retirement from Gazala in full swing this brigade was allotted a sector in the perimeter of Tobruk. On the morning of June 20th, a full panzer division, covered by heavy air forces and followed closely by lorried infantry, burst through the minefield and fell on the Camerons, Mahrattas and 2/7th Gurkhas. Less than a dozen men from 11th Brigade escaped.

5th Brigade hurried from Palestine to meet Eighth Army withdrawing over the Egyptian frontier. It came under command of 10 Ind. Div., and was allotted the key sector in the perimeter of Mersa Matruh. The enemy swept by and isolated that tiny seaport, leaving the garrison to be destroyed at leisure. Whereupon the breakout from Benghazi was re-enacted but on a large scale. On the night of June 28th, under a full moon and with the flames of Mersa Matruh in the background, small groups of vehicles began to filter through the German leaguers. For two nights and a day, in bold and chancey fashion, these little parties squirmed through the four German divisions which lay in their path. Each hour was crowned by fantastic adventure but on June

30th most of 5th Brigade reported in at El Alamein, where General Auchinleck was in personal charge of the defence. 1/4th Essex, which had replaced the Buffs, went at once to join ROBCOL on Ruweisat Ridge in the stand which saved Egypt. For the first time in thirty-six days Rommel's panzers were halted, and a stopper was driven in the Alamein bottleneck. After only seven days for re-equipment, the remainder of 5th Brigade joined the Essex on Ruweisat, where it spent the summer in probing and harassing the thwarted enemy.

The tide had turned. In September, when the 4 Ind. Div. relieved the 10th on Ruweisat, and incidentally reclaimed 5th Brigade, it was obvious that General Montgomery would strike soon. His blow fell at the end of October. Like spectators on a giant ramp, 4 Ind. Div. saw the terrific attack go in on the plains beneath them. On Ruweisat as in the south, the enemy was pinned down so that he dare not send aid to his tormented forces in the north. At the crisis of the battle 5th Brigade was called upon to cut a lane in the minefields through which the British tank reserves might pass for the kill. On the night of November 3rd, behind a barrage of 400 guns, the Essex and Rajputana Rifles advanced through 8,000 yards of minefields. In the thin light of dawn, hundreds upon hundreds of British tanks came plung-

2nd PUNJAB   REGIMENT

ing through, to turn north on Rommel's rear. The capstone had been set on one of the greatest victories of modern times.

4 Ind. Div. took no part in the 1,500 mile pursuit from Alamein to Tunisia, but remained quietly if uncomfortably at Benghazi, engaged in routine tasks which the sepoys with some justice felt might have been entrusted to men of fewer battles. At the end of February the call came once more, and a fortnight later the Division was concentrated behind the Mareth line, amid flower-spangled, grassy fields, with a great mountain buttress springing out of the plain a few miles ahead. The hour of attack neared on the Mareth Line, where 4/16th Punjabs became involved in a small war of their own. To assist in the assault of the Fiftieth Northumbrian Division, the Indian Sappers and Miners bridged the Wadi Zig Zaouw in the very teeth of the enemy.

The role of the 4 Ind. Div. in this battle was to open a road through the Matmata Mountains as a supply line for the New Zealanders, who were coming up from the south. But General Tuker had an additional project in mind. When by quick rushes the road through the Matmatas had been cleared, 5th and 7th Brigades turned north along mountain tracks and arrived well in Rommel's rear, three thousand feet above the Gabes plain. Below them the battle was in full swing.

5th MAHRATTA Light Infantry

It was a race against time to descend and to close the trap. A road down the side of a canyon had to be built. The sappers worked for eighteen hours, with 1/2nd Gurkhas passing up stones in endless chains from the bottom of the ravine. The leading detachments defiled down, only to encounter New Zealand patrols on the plain. British armour had broken through twelve hours before and Rommel was in full retreat. A masterly project was foiled by the luck of war.

The enemy's next lay-back position was Wadi Akarit—Fatnassa, which in the lie of the land was almost a replica of the Mareth Line. 4 Ind. Div's., attack was mounted against Fatnassa, a queer wild system of ridges and pinnacles, with steep escarpments and narrow, twisty chimneys, which stood like a Disney drawing on the left flank of the battleground. The enemy's position was to be forced in an audacious assault along a narrow, chimney-like corridor between two escarpments. On the night of April 5th, 7th Brigade, led by 1/2nd Gurkhas, silently crept forward until the jagged silhouette of Fatnassa loomed in the darkness ahead.

In the next five hours 4 Ind. Div. won one of its most brilliant victories. Subedar Lalbahadur Thapa almost won that victory singlehanded, when with two sections of Gurkhas he cut his way to the crest of the escarpment through a sleet

The Battle Front of WADI AKARIT. The painting shows the southern escarpments of the Fatnassa Massif, point 275, and the

By Capt. Gordon Hogg.
Zemlet el Beida on the left of the vital military road to Gafsa. It was in this area that Subedar Lalbahadur Thapa won his V.C.

of fire, leaving the sangers behind thick with enemy dead. Other Gurkha companies swarmed up to seize the dominating peaks and ridges. The Royal Sussex passed through and after hard fighting turned the Wadi Akarit anti-tank ditch. Quickly off the mark, 4/6th Rajputana Rifles hurried along the narrow defile, and wormed their way into the rear of the German positions. 4/16th Punjabs stormed and consolidated the remaining high ground on the left. The enemy had to get out, and quickly. Within thirty-six hours he was in full retreat for 125 miles across the Tunisian plains to his inner keep of mountain fortresses which stood in a great semi-circle around the ports of Bizerta and Tunis.

Here on April 19th the battle began on Djebel Garci, a great naked mountain which covered the lateral communications of the enemy. The Essex cleared the lower slopes. 4/6th Rajputana Rifles pushed on upwards through a hail of fire, to come to grips with a German convict division which fought like devils. In the grain fields and pastures below, sixteen regiments of artillery stood to their guns night and day, to crash overhelming fire first on one counter-attack and then on another. With all officers down, Havildar Major Chhelu Ram of the Rajputanas took command and led the assault with a consummate gallantry which brought him the

10th BALUCH REGIMENT

Victoria Cross. Out of ammunition, the jawans met the surge of desperate Germans with showers of stones. 1/9th Gurkhas, clambering like cats, scrambled into the fray, and emerged from the melee with whirling kukris, driving the enemy ahead of them. 4/16th Punjabs advanced through the enemy barrage as though on parade, climbed the mountain and reinforced the battle line. No sterner ordeal has ever confronted 4 Ind. Div., than this three days deathlock on the bald dome of Garci.

With serried mountain ranges behind, Djebel Garci was plainly not the gateway to Tunis. But two hundred miles away, on the south-western perimeter of this vast fighting front, British First Army had found a soft spot at the approaches to Medjez el Bab. High Command took dramatic decision. On April 30th 4 Ind. Div., and Seventh Armoured Division were ordered on to the roads at four hours notice, to leave the army that had been built around them, and to cross the mountains for the knockout blow. The operation was brilliantly planned and faultlessly executed. On the night of May 5th, with hundreds of guns and a brigade of tanks in support, with twenty squadrons of fighter-bombers on tentacle, Fifth Brigade swept over the last barrier ridges, while First and Fourth British Divisions made good the shoulders of the attack. 7th Brigade poured through on to the straight road to Tunis. It was the kill. The war in Africa was over. Nor was it unfitting when the mopping up came, that among many thousand other prisoners, the Royal Sussex and 1/2nd Gurkhas should have scooped up General von Arnim, Supreme Commander of the Axis forces in Africa.

WESTERN DESERT-TUNISIA

BENGHAZI. Its capture marked the clearance of the enemy from Libya.

TRIPOLI. The famous cathedral remained undamaged.

4/16th PUNJABS in position prior to an advance during the penetration into TUNISIA.

SFAX. A tumultuous welcome greeted the victors.

SOUSSE. The Union Jack and Tricolour fly side by side.

ENFIDAVILLE. Bitterly defended by the enemy. Batteries of 25 pounders fire heavy concentrations before infantry attack.

HALFAYA PASS. Scene of 11th Brigade's critical encounter.

BARDIA, into which the enemy retired after successes by the C.I.H.

DERNA. On the airfield here 4/11th SIKHS destroyed many aircraft.

SOLLUM. Transport moves up the famous switchback.

TUNISIA. Road built through MATMATA GORGE to allow 4th Indian Division to fall on Rommel's rear.

INFANTRY advance under smoke during Tunisian campaign.

SURRENDER! General von Arnim on his way to captivity.

The END of the WAR in NORTH AFRICA.
Troops enter TUNIS.

IT IS DOUBTFUL if at this time there was a finer battle machine in the world than the 4 Ind. Div. Three years of incessant combat had hardened Britons and Indians alike into indomitable fighters, sensitive to the vagaries, instant to the necessities, of battle. The world heard much of them; Prime Minister Churchill paid them tribute in the Commons; the King-Emperor travelled to Tripoli to thank them in person, and to pin the Victoria Cross upon Subedar Lalbahadur Thapa. Throughout that summer they rested and trained patiently, once again waiting for the call which never failed to come as the war mounted in vehemence. In December they crossed into Italy, and a month later took over a sector on the Adriatic Coast. Here the mud, sleet and slush of abominable winter weather conditioned them for the ordeals to come.

4 Ind. Div. was again at full strength, for a reconstituted 11th Brigade comprised old comrades in a new 2nd Camerons, a new 2/7th Gurkhas, and the 4/6th Rajputanas, which had been replaced in 5th Brigade by their 1/6th battalion. On February 1st the 4 Ind. Div. began to move sixty-five miles to the South-West, across the Apennines, where nightly the sky was livid with flashes, and the thunder of the guns grew until the ground trembled with the shock of artillery. At the little town of Cassino, known to military scholars as a model of impregnable terrain, an American corps, with gallantry beyond praise, had tried to storm the great buttress which barred the road to Rome. Isolated frozen, battered by night and by day, handfuls of indomitable men clung to positions which they had clawed from the grip

of the enemy. When the Indians relieved these great soldiers, brigades barely mustered 400 men. Of one battalion only fifty men remained, and they were so spent that they had to be carried out on stretchers.

Such was the fearful field to which 4 Ind. Div. was now committed. The desperate position in the Anzio bridge-head impelled High Command to brook no delay. Brigadier Lovett's 7th Brigade, inured to shock, was chosen to lead the way. The attack was planned to go in from the right flank, where the Americans had gained a footing on Snakes Head Ridge. Points 593 and 444 must be stormed before a start line could be established for assault on the main objective—the mighty massif of Monastery Hill.

Now came that proud and tragic six weeks in which, for the only time in the war, the inextinguishable ardour of "Jo Hukam" failed to vouchsafe victory. On the night of February 14th the Royal Sussex surged against Point 593, to encounter paratroopers who fought with unequalled fanaticism and disregard of death in foxholes and weapon pits hidden among the rocks. Thrown back, the same battalion attacked next night and stormed their objective but through some misunderstanding were recalled. On the night of February 17th, 1/2nd Gurkhas, 1/9th Gurkhas, 4/6 Rajputanas, with the Rajputana Machine Gun Battalion in close

support, came forward and flung themselves at the high ground. In a melee even fiercer than Garci, the Rajputanas took and lost Point 593. The Gurkha battalions swept forward across minefields under an unparalleled blaze of mortar bombs, grenades and spandau fire, in a great bid to win the supreme prize of Monastery Hill. Two thirds of 1/2nd Gurkhas were down in ten minutes yet the survivors battled on, leaving their dead far up on the slopes of the final objective. The attack failed, for the task was more than men born of women could encompass. Not only the infantry and artillery (11th Field Regiment in particular) paid toll in this maelstrom of battle; every service lost heavily. During the battle Subedar Subramanyan, a Madrassi sapper, covered a mine with his body to save his comrades and posthumously received the George Cross.

It was March 15th before a second attack could be mounted. On that date 5th Brigade, together with the New Zealand Division, attempted to reach Monastery Hill by first clearing the town of Cassino which lay, a heap of broken masonry, in the shadow of the great buttress. Once again fighting rose to a crescendo of unbelievable bitterness. The Essex held Castle Hill, while 1/6th Rajputanas joined the Kiwis in bitter and fluctuating fighting on the lower slopes. Two nights later 1/9th Gurkhas won imperishable fame in one of the greatest

exploits of the war. They stormed Hangman's Hill and for seven days and nights beat off the enemies who had closed in a ring around them. Those who lived were finally withdrawn when the operation was abandoned as hopeless.

For the 4 Ind. Div. as for many other fine divisions, Cassino was Gethsemane. Here passed the last of the old hands. Withdrawn to the Adriatic Coast the Division entered an unpleasant sector and gradually took over a wide front. The breakthrough on the Rapido in April led to an enemy withdrawal. Early in June 4 Ind. Div. was briefed for pursuit and followed up the retreat, mopping up rearguards and liberating Chieti, Pescara and Citta San Angelo. In this advance 149th Anti-tank Regiment distinguished itself by the speed with which it overcame obstacles and kept its screen ahead of the rapidly moving infantry. After relief by the Poles, the division returned to Campobasso for training. A trek into Central Italy followed, for the Germans after the loss of Rome were ending their long retreat in the mountainous terrain between Lake Trasimeno and the Tiber. Here on July 8th, with 10th Brigade of 10 Ind. Div. under command, 4 Ind. Div. joined in the arduous process of prying the Germans from their grip on the serried ridges between the valleys of the Arno and the Tiber.

14th PUNJAB REGIMENT

Five divisions (three of them Indian) battled their way forward on a front of sixty-five miles. 4 Ind. Div. jumping off from west of Umbertide, stormed Alvieri Ridge, and pushed forward on a two brigade front. On July 13th in the San Maria di Tiberina and Cedrone areas, severe fighting ensued. The spread of the Tiber valley altered the Divisional axis from north to west. Thereafter the advance lay against the grain of the ground, giving greater observation to the enemy ensconced on the heights above, and markedly increasing difficulties on a battlefield almost completely devoid of roads. East of Arezzo the Divisional engineers built "Jacob's Ladder", a jeep track of outstanding ingenuity. It was in this area that Lieut. St. J. G. Young and Sowar Ditto Ram proved their blood brotherhood with Subedar Subramanyan who also gave his life on a minefield, to win the Division's second and third George Crosses. After the fall of Arezzo the axis of advance again altered to the north, and by early August the enemy was backed against the mighty spine of the Apennines. An attack on the massive Gothic Line loomed ahead.

On August 23rd, 4 Ind. Div. began to move into position for that attack by concentrating behind a screen of Italian troops near Fossato, on the eastern slopes of the High Appenines. Here the enemy thinly covered his main Gothic Line position thirty miles ahead. 5th Brigade led a brilliant

movement conducted at great speed, which in four days carried the Divisional front up to the hinge of the main Gothic Line position in front of Urpino and provided flank protection for the projected Eighth Army attack. In this advance 2/11th Sikhs marched 36 hours with only six hours halt, outdistancing their supplies and living on tomatoes and corn cobs from the fields. This rapid advance brought the Indian troops into the battle zone ahead of the German reserves, and enabled them to secure dominating ridges for their start line in the great Eighth Army assault, which began on the morning of August 31st.

In this great attack 5th and 11th Brigades were the first Allied troops to break into the main Gothic Line positions. 3/10th Baluchis and 4/11th Sikhs stormed Monte Calvo, and 11th Brigade exploited the gain to Tavoleto, where the Camerons, 2/7th Gurkhas and 2/11th Sikhs fought bitterly to secure Monte San Giovanni, a high razor-backed feature above the valley of the Conca. 7th Brigade passed through and 1/2nd Gurkhas seized Auditore. 11th Brigade turned into the east to rid flanking British divisions of Gemmano. The attack then switched nearly due west, where the high buttress of San Marino, the tiny city republic, towered above the countryside. 5th Brigade pushed through 46th British

Division front, taking Montescudo. Faetano crossing on the Marano was bitterly contested but 1/9th Gurkhas, in the grim setting of the village cemetery, destroyed the garrison in deadly hand to hand combat. Here Rifleman Sher Bahadur Thapa by his daring and cold courage brought his battalion its first Victoria Cross. Following up swiftly, the Camerons stole into San Marino in a silent night attack which won that citadel with negligible losses.

The Rimini Line was broken and the pace quickened. On September 23rd, 2/7th Gurkhas and 3/12th Frontier Force Regiment, which had replaced 4/6th Rajputanas in 11th Brigade, forced the Marecchia crossing after heavy fighting. 7th Brigade's time-tried team, Royal Sussex and 1/2nd Gurkhas, took up the running and encountered intense opposition at Reggione, just short of the insignificant stream which bears the famous name of Rubicon. After a diversionary move to the east to relieve pressure on 46th British Division, 4 Ind. Div. handed over its responsibilities to 10 Ind. Div.

This advance across twenty-five miles of country defended by first class infantry with great weight of artillery and armour in support, must be counted among 4 Ind. Div's. finest achievements. Yard by yard these great fighting men smashed, probed and infiltrated through the strongest

defences. The new units kept the pledge of "Jo Hukam" in the same indomitable spirit as their predecessors. The Division moved to rest in anticipation of rejoining Eighth Army for the final overthrow of the enemy in Italy. At Perugia, as at Sidi Barrani, as at Keren, as at Enfidaville, dramatic news arrived. Greece was about to be liberated. The 4 Ind. Div. would proceed there at once.

The story of Greece is a tale of its own, to which there may yet be something to add. The 4 Ind. Div. (7th Brigade at Salonika, 11th Brigade at Patras, 5th Brigade at Athens) arrived in the bountiful hours of liberation. But parochial dissensions and hates quickly stilled the paeans of gratitude, and it became sadly evident that there existed an organisation in Greece prepared to use force to gain political ends and to suppress democratic liberties. British and Indian soldiers were committed to a battle which had no meaning to them, in order that the rule of law and liberty might prevail. Tragedies followed, as always in war, but tragedies now highlighted by brutalities Nazi in their grossness, barbaric in their stupidity. During this trying period, the men of the 4 Ind. Div. bore themselves with exemplary patience and forbearance. When the truce of Varkiza was signed the Division mustered in Macedonia Ibrace to guarantee peace among the

polyglot population of the feverish northern frontiers.

Administrators, public servants extraordinary, guardians and mentors of national authority—such were the final roles in Europe of men dedicated to as many battles as Napoleon's Guard ever knew. Yet whether in the glare of the desert, on bitter mountain crest, at river crossing, or among malarial Macedonian villages, the Fourth Indian Division's steadfast pledge remains its pride, "Jo Hukam".

"Whatever thing is required, that thing will we do".

BATTLE FOR CASSINO. The gunners maintain heavy concentrations by day and night.

CASSINO MASSIF, with the VALLEY of the RAPIDO in the foreground.

CASSINO...HANGMAN'S HILL, a feature which juts out from the side of Monastery Hill. Held by units of Gurkha, Essex and Rajputana regts.

CASSINO. THE MONASTERY from Snakes Head Ridge. Attacked by Sussex, Rajputana and Gurkha Regts. Feb. 15th — 18th 1944.

CHIETI — the main square after liberation.

PESCARA RIVER— bridged by sappers.

PESCARA. Part of the ruined town.

PERUGIA. It was here the Division received orders for move to Greece.

AREZZO. East of the town the sappers built "Jacobs Ladder".

SHELL TORN buildings on MONTE CALVO in the Gothic Line. Stormed by Baluchis and Sikhs.

RUINED TAVOLETO. Stormed by 2/7th Gurkhas in unrehearsed attack. Bitter fighting took place here.

GEMMANO (with San Marino top left) captured after eleven previous attacks.

THE FALL OF SAN MARINO. The actual assault on the citadel. Ultimately taken in a night attack by the Camerons.

SAN MARINO with its three pinnacles. In foreground FAETANO, where Sher Bahadur Thapa won his V.C.

FREEDOM AT SALONIKA, where 4th Indian Division re-established Greek Government authority.

TROOPS VIEW THE ACROPOLIS.

INDIAN DIVISIONS WON A FINE REPUTATION IN WORLD WAR TWO

Field Marshal Auchinleck, Commander-in-Chief of the British Indian Army from 1942, asserted that the British *"couldn't have come through both wars (World War I and II) if they hadn't had the British Indian Army"*. British Prime Minister Winston Churchill also paid tribute to *"the unsurpassed bravery of Indian soldiers and officers"*.

Between 1945 and 1947, the Director of Public Relations, War Department, Government of India, published a series of short publications covering the individual histories of the WWII Indian Divisions. They followed a consistent format, having between 44 and 48 pages within illustrated soft card covers. They have an average of 50 monochrome photographic illustrations, and each has a full colour centrespread depicting a scene from the Division's wartime operations (drawn by official war artists). They were printed at various presses in Bombay and New Delhi, and each contains at least one map.

As condensed histories they are useful – particularly those which relate to Divisions for which no other record was ever produced.

The British Indian Army during World War II began the war, in 1939, numbering just under 200,000 men. By the end of the war, it had become the largest volunteer army in history, rising to over 2.5 million men in August 1945. Serving in divisions of infantry, armour and a fledgling airborne force, they fought on three continents: in Africa, Europe and Asia.

This Army fought in Ethiopia against the Italian Army, in Egypt, Libya, Tunisia and Algeria against both the Italian and German Army and, after the Italian surrender, against the German Army in Italy. However, the bulk of the British Indian Army was committed to fighting the Japanese Army, first during the British defeats in Malaya and the retreat from Burma to the Indian border; later, after resting and refitting for the victorious advance back into Burma, as part of the largest British Empire army ever formed. These campaigns cost the lives of over 87,000 Indian service- men, while another 34,354 were wounded, and 67,340 became prisoners of war. Their valour was recognised with the award of some 4,000 decorations, and 18 members of the British Indian Army were awarded the Victoria Cross or the George Cross.

RED EAGLES
The Story of the 4th Indian Division
9781474537520

During the Second World War, the 4th Indian Division was in the vanguard of nine campaigns in the Mediterranean theatre, Egypt, Eritrea, Syria, Tunisia, Italy and Greece. The 4th Division captured 150,000 prisoners and suffered 25,000 casualties, more than the strength of a whole division. It won over 1,000 honours and awards, which included four Victoria Crosses and three George Crosses. Field Marshal Lord Wavell wrote: "The fame of this Division will surely go down as one of the greatest fighting formations in military history."

THE FIGHTING FIFTH
History of the 5th Indian Division
9781474537513

As described in much greater detail in Anthony Brett James's book 'The Ball of Fire', the division saw active service in East Africa, North Africa and Burma.

GOLDEN ARROW
The Story of the 7th Indian Division
9781474537506

The role of this division is also duplicated by a much larger work: the book by Brig. M. R. Roberts. However, this booklet gives a good account of Kohima and Imphal and the crossing of the Irrawaddy. In 1945, the division was flown into Siam, so becoming the first Allied formation to re-enter South East Asia.

ONE MORE RIVER
The Story of the 8th Indian Division
Biferno, Trigno, Sangro, Moro, Rapido, Arno, Senio, Santerno, Po, Adige

9781474537490

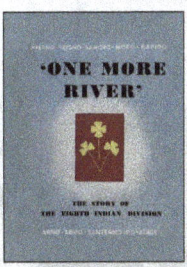

The 8th Indian Division started its overseas service in the Middle East in the garrisoning of Iraq and then the invasion of Persia to secure the oil fields of the area for the Allies, before moving to Italy in 1943. Landing at Taranto, it pushed up the length of the peninsula in a series of major battles: breaking the Sangro Line, forcing the Rapido and turning the defences at Cassino, breaking the stubborn German resistance at Monte Grande and, finally, forcing the Po River. It won four VCs, 26 DSOs and 149 MCs along the way. During the war the 8th Indian Division sustained casualties totalling 2,012 dead, 8,189 wounded and 749 missing.

BLACK CAT DIVISION
17th Indian Division

9781474537483

This formation was committed to Burma from the early days when the British were in full flight from the invading Japanese. It remained in Burma right through to the end, when the starving remnants of the Japanese Army were making their own desperate retreat.

TIGER HEAD
The Story of the 26th Indian Division
Arakan, Ragoon

9781474537452

This is a history of the division said later by the Japanese to have been the opponent which they most feared. The 26th held the Allied monsoon line in the Arakan during two such seasons, repulsing every attack launched against it. Later it made a series of leap-frog landings down the coast to clinch the issue in the Arakan. It was the first division to enter Ragoon, invading the city from the sea.

A HAPPY FAMILY
The Story of the Twentieth Indian Division, April 1942-August 1945
9781474537476

One of the few Indian divisions in the 14th Army trained specifically for the war in Burma. Raised in Bangalore in 1942, it commenced active operations in late 1943 and served from Imphal through to the end. It established the 14th Army's first brigade-head across the Chindwin and its second such brigade-head across the Irrawaddy. Its final task was to round up the Japanese in French Indochina.

THE TWENTY THIRD INDIAN DIVISION
"The Fighting Cock Division"
Burma, Malaya, Java
9781474537469

The Fighting Cock Division is well recorded in the book by Doulton. This book gives coverage of the heavy fighting at the Kohima Battle, the capture of Tamu, the reoccupation of Malaya in August 1945, and then its strange role on the island of Java – concurrently disarming the Japanese garrison, fighting the insurgent Indonesian nationalists, and caring for 65,000 former internees pending the arrival of a new Dutch administration.

TEHERAN TO TRIESTE
The Story Of The Tenth Indian Division
9781783317028

This History deals with the 10th Indian Div's exploits in Iraq (under Maj Gen "Bill" Slim) its role in the Libyan battles leading up to El Alamein, the following two years of garrison duties in Cyprus and Syria, and finally, its fighting services in the Italian campaign (from Ortona onwards).

THE STORY OF THE 25th INDIAN DIVSION
The Arakan Campaign
9781783317585

Formed in Southern India in August 1942 for defence of that area in case of Japanese invasion, the "Ace of Spades" Division had its baptism of fire in Arakan in February 1944. It served throughout the remainder of that campaign the climax being the battle of Tamandu.

Its victorious fight for the Kangaw roadblock was considered by many to have been the fiercest battle of the entire Burma war, while its liberation of Akyab was the first convincing proof to the rest of the world that the tide had turned against the Japanese.

DAGGER DIVISION
The Story Of The 19th Indian Division
9781783317035

Raised in the late 1941, the 19th was the first "standard" Indian Division. Its troops were the first to breach the Japanese defence line in Burma and to raise the flag at Fort Dufferin. It crossed the Chindwin in November 1944, driving on to Mandalay and Ragoon during seven months of continuous fighting. The 19th's exploits are graphically described also in John Masters' personal memoir, *The Road Past Mandalay*.

www.ingramcontent.com/pod-product-compliance
Lightning Source LLC
Chambersburg PA
CBHW041928090426
42743CB00021B/3476